Slaughter in the Mud

The Canadians at Passchendaele, 1917

by

N.M. Christie

The Access to History Series
Number 4

CEF BOOKS
1998

"Access to History; The Canadian History Series:
Number 4"
Slaughter in the Mud: The Canadians at Passchendaele
ISBN 1-896979-12-2

Published by: CEF BOOKS
                 P.O. 29123
                 3500 Fallowfield Road
                 Nepean, Ontario, K2J 4A9.

Editor-in-Chief: R.B. McClean

Access to History; The Canadian History Series

Acknowledgements:
We would like to thank the Royal Canadian Legion Ontario Command branches for the support that made this book possible.

This book is dedicated to the memory of the Canadians who willingly gave their lives in the defence of freedom in the Twentieth Century. Lest We Forget.

Maps by Constable Enterprises, Stittsville, Ontario.
Graphics and Layout by Imágenes Graphic Arts, Ottawa, Ontario.

Front cover: The Front Line; Members of the 16th Canadian Machine Gun Company at Passchendaele. (PAC PA2162).

Printed in Canada

"You know Hughie, this is suicide."

**The final words of Talbot Papineau,
October 30th, 1917.**

EUROPE 1914-1918

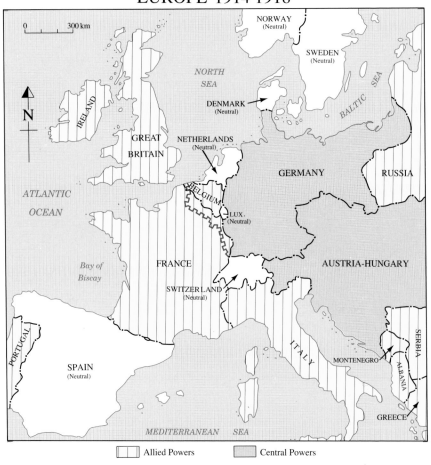

TABLE OF CONTENTS

GENERAL TRENCH-LINE
ON THE WESTERN FRONT
1914-1918

INTRODUCTION

More than any other battle, Passchendaele illustrates the horror and the futility that characterized the First World War. It was fought in a sea of mud where men attacked in unfathomable conditions for reasons which are difficult to grasp. Throughout the three and one-half months of the battle, the soldiers of the British Empire struggled as much against the thick, waist-deep mud as they did against the determined German defenders.

To reach the enemy positions, the assault troops were forced to wade through the dense muck. Exhausted artillerymen had to haul their heavy guns through the quagmire only to toil for hours constructing platforms that would prevent the guns from sinking. Even in death, there was no respite from the mud. Thousands of wounded soldiers fell into the ooze and disappeared. And through it all, the Germans had the enormous advantage of occupying the highlands of Passchendaele Ridge from which they could rain murderous fire down on the helpless attackers. For the men of the British Empire, Passchendaele was hell on earth.

When the Canadians arrived to take their turn in the meat grinder in late October 1917, the battle of Passchendaele had already raged for almost three months. The original British objective to secure the heights surrounding beleaguered Ypres and to break through to the German-controlled, channel ports had been abandoned. Instead, the campaign had degenerated into a hideous war of attrition. In the process, the British and Australians had incurred 250,000 casualties for an advance of only 5,500 metres. It was now up to the Canadians to capture the elusive Passchendaele Ridge and, by so doing, salvage British respectability.

In the autumn of 1917, the Canadians were known as "Byng's Boys", the Canadians of Vimy, the most successful Corps in the British army. Experienced, organized and proud, they had worked hard to achieve their reputation as the best storm troops. Time and again, they had succeeded where others had failed. Already in 1917, they had won resounding victories at Vimy Ridge, Arleux, Fresnoy and Hill 70. Now, at Passchendaele, they faced a most formidable challenge.

For the few Canadian veterans who had survived the terrible fighting in the Ypres Salient during 1915 and 1916, the terrain was now unrecognizable. The city of Ypres had been obliterated by continuous bombardment and the surrounding farmland was a morass of deep mud, shell holes and rotting corpses. The sweet-sickly smell of the dead pervaded the air. All the lush greenery of earlier days was gone and only splinters remained where forests had once stood. In their place was a scene of utter desolation.

In the end, the Canadians would overcome the impassable landscape and the tenacious German resistance to achieve a victory few thought possible. Sparked by a series of individual feats of bravery, the Canadian Corps would capture and hold the heights of Passchendaele Ridge. However, it would require three weeks of dreadful fighting, and the full resources of the 100,000 men of the Canadian Corps, to advance the 2,000 metres necessary to secure the Passchendaele highlands. Along this road of bitter triumph, 5,000 Canadians would die.

Ruins of the Cloth Hall, Ypres, July 1916 (PAC PA314)

The Strong Arms of Canada

COMPONENTS OF THE CANADIAN CORPS
PASSCHENDAELE 1917

1ST INFANTRY BRIGADE	2ND INFANTRY BRIGADE	3RD INFANTRY BRIGADE
1ST BATTALION (WESTERN ONTARIO)	5TH BATTALION (SASKATCHEWAN)	13TH BATTALION (BLACK WATCH OF MONTREAL)
2ND BATTALION (EASTERN ONTARIO)	7TH BATTALION (BRITISH COLUMBIA)	14TH BATTALION (ROYAL MONTREAL REGIMENT)
3RD BATTALION (TORONTO REGIMENT)	8TH BATTALION (90TH RIFLES OF WINNIPEG)	15TH BATTALION (48TH HIGHLANDERS WINNIPEG)
4TH BATTALION (CENTRAL ONTARIO)	10TH BATTALION (ALBERTA)	16TH BATTALION (CANADIAN SCOTTISH)

2ND CANADIAN DIVISION

4TH INFANTRY BRIGADE	5TH INFANTRY BRIGADE	6TH INFANTRY BRIGADE
18TH BATTALION (WESTERN ONTARIO)	22ND BATTALION (CANADIEN-FRANCAIS	27TH BATTALION (CITY OF WINNIPEG)
19TH BATTALION (CENTRAL ONTARIO)	24TH BATTALION (VICTORIA RIFLES OF MONTREAL)	28TH BATTALION (SASKATCHEWAN)
20TH BATTALION (CENTRAL ONTARIO)	25TH BATTALION (NOVA SCOTIA)	29TH BATTALION (BRITISH COLUMBIA)
21ST BATTALION (EASTERN ONTARIO)	26TH BATTALION (NEW BRUNSWICK)	31ST BATTALION (ALBERTA)

3RD CANADIAN DIVISION

7TH INFANTRY BRIGADE	8TH INFANTRY BRIGADE	9TH INFANTRY BRIGADE
ROYAL CANADIAN REGIMENT *(NOVA SCOTIA)*	1ST CANADIAN MOUNTED RIFLES *(SASKATCHEWAN)*	43RD BATTALION *(CAMERON HIGHLANDERS OF WINNIPEG)*
PRINCESS PATRICIA'S CANADIAN LIGHT INFANTRY *(EASTERN ONTARIO)*	2ND CANADIAN MOUNTED RIFLES *(BRITISH COLUMBIA)*	52ND BATTALION *(NEW ONTARIO)*
42ND BATTALION *(BLACK WATCH OF MONTREAL)*	4TH CANADIAN MOUNTED RIFLES *(CENTRAL ONTARIO)*	58TH BATTALION *(CENTRAL ONTARIO)*
49TH BATTALION *(ALBERTA)*	5TH CANADIAN MOUNTED RIFLES *(QUEBEC)*	116TH BATTALION *(ONTARIO COUNTY)*

4TH CANADIAN DIVISION

10TH INFANTRY BRIGADE	11TH INFANTRY BRIGADE	12TH INFANTRY BRIGADE
44TH BATTALION *(MANITOBA)*	54TH BATTALION *(BRITISH COLUMBIA)*	38TH BATTALION *(EASTERN ONTARIO)*
46TH BATTALION *(SASKATCHEWAN)*	75TH BATTALION *(MISSISSAUGA HORSE)*	72ND BATTALION *(SEAFORTH HIGHLANDERS OF VANCOUVER)*
47TH BATTALION *(BRITISH COLUMBIA)*	87TH BATTALION *(GRENADIER GUARDS OF MONTREAL)*	78TH BATTALION *(WINNIPEG GRENADIERS)*
50TH BATTALION *(ALBERTA)*	102ND BATTALION *(NORTH BRITISH)*	85TH BATTALION *(NOVA SCOTIA HIGHLANDERS)*

THE MAKE-UP OF AN ARMY

The Army - The British Forces on the Western Front were divided into 4 or 5 Armies. The British Army in the field was commanded by Field Marshall Sir Douglas Haig. Throughout the war the British Army varied in strength, but usually employed 4,000,000 (1917) soldiers in the field. The Canadian Corps belonged to the 1st British Army, but had stints with the 4th Army as well.

The Army Corps - An Army Corps consisted of a number of Infantry Divisions, depending on its needs. The Corps was commanded by a Lieutenant-General. Its numeric strength varied, but could put as many as 120,000 men in the field. The Canadian Corps was made-up of 4 Divisions, all Canadian, but often had British Divisions attached for special attacks or battles.

The Division - The Infantry Division was composed of 3 Infantry Brigades and had 20,000 soldiers. It was commanded by a Major-General. The make-up of the 20,000 soldiers included 12,000 infantry, 3,500 artillerymen, 750 in a medical section, and 2,000 engineers and pioneers.

The Brigade - The Infantry Brigade was commanded by a Brigadier-General and consisted of 4 Battalions (4,000 infantrymen). Each Brigade had Engineers, signals, a field ambulance, trench mortar unit and machine gun unit.

The Battalion - The Infantry Battalion consisted of 1,000 men. This was the theoretical strength of the unit, after headquarters staff, illness, wounded, etc. were deducted, a Battalion would normally put 650 rifles into the line. It was commanded by a Lieutenant-Colonel. Each Battalion was made-up of 4 companies (200 men), commanded by a Major or Captain. In turn, the company was broken into 4 platoons commanded by a Lieutenant and each platoon into 4 sections commanded by a sergeant.

Slaughter in the Mud

The Canadians at Passchendaele

October-November, 1917

HISTORICAL OVERVIEW

The Canadian attacks on the Passchendaele Ridge in late October and early November of 1917 capped a major British offensive that had commenced amid buoyant expectations on July 31st of that year. The fighting on the Bellevue Spur and the capture of Passchendeale village, which represented the Canadian contributions to the lengthy battle, have become known officially as the 8th Battle of the Third Battle of Ypres.

The British High Command's objective in this offensive was to break through the German defences in the Ypres Salient, seize the highlands of Passchendaele Ridge and capture the German-occupied, Belgian channel ports. Unfortunately, as with most battles of the First World War, the objectives were beyond the capabilities of the strategists and the armies. British, French, New Zealand, Australian and finally Canadian troops were thrown against the German defences in the most harrowing conditions with little hope of success. By the time the offensive closed down, few of the hoped for outcomes were realized and more than 250,000 British Empire soldiers were dead, wounded or missing for a gain of less than 7,000 metres.

The Passchendaele offensive began with great optimism at 3:50 a.m. on July 31st, 1917. Initially, the British attacks radiating eastward from Ypres met with success. Troops, advancing more than 2,000 metres, secured Pilkem village and drove northeast towards Langemarck and St. Julien. However, the Germans immediately counter-attacked and recaptured some of the hard-won territory. In the southern area of attack, Hooge and Bellewaerde Ridge fell, and the British regained important ground lost in 1915. Nevertheless, the Germans, keenly aware of the strategic value of the Ypres area, stiffened their resistance and over the next few days managed to stop the British in their tracks.

At this point, the British High Command encountered a new enemy. After the initial attack, the Flanders Plain experienced torrential rain for three days and the drainage system, which had been destroyed by the artillery barrages of previous battles, was unable to dissipate the water. As a result, the low-lying region of the Ypres Salient became a sea of mud. Over the duration of the battle, the amount of rain remained abnormally high and the millions of exploding shells further exacerbated the condition of the terrain by repeatedly churning the mud until it was waist deep in most places. For the soldiers of the British Empire, the endless mud became as much an enemy as their German adversaries.

Despite the gruesome conditions, the British High Command was determined to push the battle forward. For the next two weeks, a series of localized attacks produced some small gains, but it was not until August 16th that a determined assault was renewed. During the next two days, the British successfully captured the pulverized remains of the villages of Langemarck and St. Julien. Thereafter, progress was slow, although respectable by First World War standards, but the expected breakthrough to the channel ports was not forthcoming. A combination of the exhausting mud and German control of the higher ground from which they could rain accurate artillery fire on the helpless attackers proved too much and the momentum of the attack was again lost. For the British, it had been a bittersweet beginning to the Battle of Passchendaele or the Third Battle of Ypres, as it was officially known; some of the territory lost during the first German gas attacks of 1915 was recaptured, but, during the fighting from July 31st to the end of August, the British army had also suffered 70,800 casualties.

After a period of regrouping and refitting, the next major assault was launched on September 20th when the British High Command decided to exploit the successes in the southern section of the Ypres Salient. At 5:40 a.m. on that day, British and Australian troops attacked in the general direction of Zonnebeke. Between September 20th and 25th, along ground churned into a morass by heavy rain and incessant shellfire, the armies drove against the German positions along the Menin road. On September 26th, when the charred remains of Polygon Wood and debris that had been the town of Zonnebeke fell to the relentless onslaught, German morale appeared to be faltering. However, the British and Australians had incurred another 35,000 casualties between September 20th and October 3rd.

A breakthrough seemed possible when the attack was once again renewed on October 4th. Overcoming the sapping mud, the New Zealanders stormed the Abraham Heights and captured the strategic

Gravenstafel Ridge. Australian patrols actually entered Passchendaele village, the highest point on the Passchendaele Ridge, but were forced to withdraw because they had insufficient numbers to hold the village.

With a foothold on Passchendaele Ridge, the men of the British Empire now planned to exploit these hard-won and drier positions. On October 9th, and again on October 12th, British, Australian and New Zealand soldiers desperately tried to breech the German lines and achieve the desired breakthrough. However, faced with disaster, the faltering Germans recovered and the Australians and New Zealanders were stopped by a combination of barbed-wire, massive artillery bombardments and vicious machine-gun fire. With the rejuvenated German defence, the successes of late September and October 4th disappeared in the cruel mud of Flanders. The offensive was spent, the weather was worsening and the fabled breakthrough still existed on paper only. For their massive losses, the British armies had failed to capture Passchendaele Ridge and the channel ports remained elusively distant. In spite of these concerns, the British High Command, with its reputation at stake, decided to continue the campaign. This time the Canadian Corps would be fed to the mud and the guns.

THE YPRES SALIENT AND THE SIGNIFICANCE OF PASSCHENDAELE RIDGE

Ypres is an ancient city located on the flat Flanders Plain in the extreme western part of Belgium. Although it held no particular strategic value during the First World War, it was of great political importance. In 1914, the Germans, guided by their Schlieffen Plan, attacked France by way of Belgium. While the invasion was halted at the Marne River and Paris saved, most of Belgium was occupied by the German army. Only the area around Ypres was all that remained of Belgium. For this reason, the Allies, intent on keeping the last bit of Belgium free, were prepared to defend Ypres at all costs.

The desperate fighting around Ypres in 1914 and 1915 had produced a bulge or salient in the British line that protruded into German-held territory. It was at the "Ypres salient" in 1915 that poison gas had first been used with deadly effect against the French and the Canadians. By 1917, German successes had not only reduced the size of the salient, but had also reworked the perimeter so that it followed a semi-circular pattern extending about 5,000 metres into the German front-lines.

The Ypres salient was one of the most dangerous places on the entire Western Front. The bulge in the front-line enabled the Germans to fire into the British positions from in front and both sides. It was a "hot" place and every soldier dreaded being in the lines there. The salient was also vulnerable to a major German attack. At any time, the Germans, attacking from the north and south, could attempt to pinch-off any troops in the bulge. If they were successful in cutting off the British positions from behind, there would be no avenue of escape for the thousands of trapped soldiers.

The Germans also had the advantage of topography on their side. The Ypres salient was located on the Flanders Plain, an area distinguished by flat, low-lying agricultural land with few heights of any significance. Occasionally, the land rose to form almost imperceptible ridges. Control of these ridges was of great military importance, for they offered the occupier the "eyes" to observe all the opponent's movements and to direct deadly artillery fire accurately on the enemy's positions. In the summer of 1917, unfortunately for the British, the Germans controlled virtually all of the high positions in the Ypres salient.

The most prominent of these crests of land was Passchendaele Ridge which ran in a crescent-shape about eight kilometres east of Ypres. It was a truly dominating position. The Germans, aware of its crucial importance, had turned the entire ridge into an armed bastion. For the British, their precarious position in the Ypres salient could only be alleviated by seizing Passchendaele Ridge. Once the Ridge was captured, the British could then utilize the high ground to harass the surrounding German positions and to launch a decisive attack on the German-occupied channel ports. These ports were important to the German war strategy, as many of their deadly submarines operated from them.

THE GERMAN DEFENCES

In mid-October, the Canadian Corps was given the dubious task of securing Passchendaele Ridge. Immediately, the Canadians set about devising a strategy that would defeat the mud and allow them to penetrate the formidable German defences. The German defensive system reflected the unique conditions found in the Ypres salient. The high water table precluded the use of the traditional trench systems that were employed in other sectors of the Western Front like the Somme and Vimy. In their place, the Germans erected a complex system of interlocking

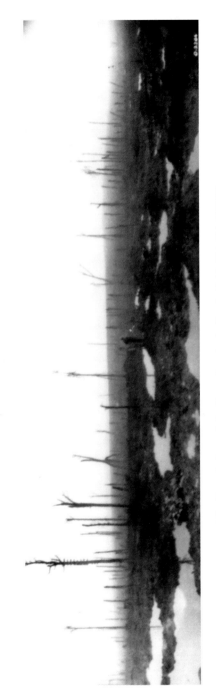

The Desolation of the Passchendaele Battlefield (PA PA40139)

pillboxes. S.G. Bennett, historian of the 4th Canadian Rifles, describes the problems encountered when attacking the German defensive lines as follows:

"The enemy's line of defence was not a series of uniform trenches to be taken and mopped up. Instead there were isolated trenches and strong-points dotted here and there. The greatest obstacles were the pill-boxes. They were manned by picked resistance-troops who fought with courage and resolution, keeping their rifles and machine-guns in action until bombed or bayoneted. Only by collective bravery and individual acts of gallantry were these obstacles removed. Contrary to popular belief the majority of pill-boxes were not loop-holed fortresses from which the defenders fought. They were square rooms of reinforced-concrete with walls and roof about five feet thick with one door in the rear leading into a fire-trench. Their walls were too thick to allow a field of fire through ports. During a bombardment and when not in action the garrison gained shelter within, but as soon as an attack was launched, the occupants manned the fire-trench which ran behind and extended on either side of the pill-box. They took the place of deep dug-outs, which were impracticable in such a low-lying country, and were good rallying points giving moral support to the defenders.

"They were formidable, but with one weakness, their range of fire was limited, and unless covered by other pill-boxes on the flanks the blind points in the range of fire made it possible for individual attackers to crawl up under cover and bomb the garrison behind. This explains many of the individual acts of heroism in capturing or demolishing a crew defending a pillbox."

THE CONDITION OF THE BATTLEFIELD

During the summer of 1917, the battered Flanders Plain had its typical dose of heavy precipitation. However, a combination of torrential down-pours during August and the expenditure of millions of artillery shells further exacerbated the nightmarish conditions. The intricate drainage system, which had been constructed over the centuries, had been destroyed by prolonged artillery fire during three years of fighting The water, having no place to drain, collected in the low-lying areas and the incessant shell-fire churned earth and water into a quagmire. As a result, the worst battlefield conditions known to man were in effect. The entire Ypres salient became a sea of oozing, yellow mud, at depths which slowed movement to a crawl and threatened to drown the soldiers who waded through the morass. The thousands of rotting corpses littering the battlefield accentuated the horror.

Movement could only take place at night, out of sight of the spotters for the German artillery, who had the enormous advantage of being positioned on the high ground. The men moved to and from the front-lines on wooden tracks called bathmats or duckboards, laid and continuously maintained by soldiers and pioneers. It was the only way to cross the muddy ooze; off the tracks, the men could barely move. The Germans, aware of these tenuous links, shelled the duckboards intermittently, killing men and horses transporting munitions and supplies to the front.

At Passchendaele, the Canadian troops launched their attacks close to dawn, following a carefully-timed, protective artillery barrage. Soldiers, heavily laden with rifles, ammunition, shovels and other accoutrements of war, rose from their shell holes or ditch-like trenches and moved sluggishly toward the German lines. Slowed by mud, at times one metre deep, they often lost the coverage of their barrage and fell victim to German counter-battery and machine-gun fire. Where possible, the wounded were evacuated quickly from the action, but many of those immobilized by their injuries drowned in the merciless ooze.

For the six Canadian battalions that wore kilts into battle, the struggle against the mud took a cruel turn. The heavy skirts became coated in mud adding extra weight and discomfort to the soldiers. When the mud dried, the hem of the kilt tore at the legs as it swayed back and forth causing wounds that often festered. Nor was there any respite from the horrific conditions during the calmer periods either before or after an attack. Sleep was almost impossible, food rations were frequently in short supply, and hordes of rats, fattened from feasting on the decomposing corpses, were a constant plague to the men. Clearly, the hardships of the Ypres salient were beyond just the bullets and the shells.

ENTER THE CANADIANS

C ommanded now by a Canadian, Sir Arthur Currie, the Canadian Corps was having a successful year. Although 1917 was the bleakest year of the war for the Allies, it was one triumph after another for the Canadians. The Corps had orchestrated a series of stunning victories at Vimy, Arleux, Fresnoy and Hill 70 and, in the process, had developed a reputation for success, efficiency and planning. Passchendaele, however, would be a crushing test of the much heralded Canadian capabilities. Initially, Currie was reluctant to accept the Canadian role in continuing the offensive. He saw no strategic reason to expend lives in the capture of Passchendaele. His objections were overruled, but he did win a delay in starting the attack until his Canadians were completely ready.

Canadians Pioneers Laying Trench Mats, November 1917 (PAC PA2156)

THE PLAN

The overall aim of the Canadian attack was to secure a defensible position on Passchendaele Ridge. The Canadians adopted a simple plan to achieve this goal. Instead of making one all out push towards Passchendaele Ridge, they would move towards it through a series of carefully planned attacks, each with a limited objective. The mud had rendered most of the low-lying ground impassable and the decision was made to launch the attacks from higher ground. Unfortunately, the only two jump-off points that matched the Canadian requirements were the footing the Australians had won at the base of Passchendaele Ridge and Bellevue Spur, a small spur that ran upwards, west to east, to join the main Passchendaele Ridge. Both approaches presented a narrow front and the advancing Canadians could expect to be hammered by the German artillery.

"The condition of the ground beggars description. Just one mass of shell holes all full of water. The strongest and youngest men cannot navigate without falling down. The people we relieved tell me, in the attack, a great many of their men were drowned in shell holes for want of strength to pull themselves out when dog-tired."

Agar Adamson, P.P.C.L.I.

The Passchendaele Battlefield, October - November 1917 (PAC C31652)

Experience had taught the Canadians that success in battle was dependent on an effective transport system, wisely positioned artillery and a reliable communications network. Currie insisted that this groundwork be completed before the Canadian Corps began its step by step assault on Passchendaele Ridge. Consequently, on October 17th, Canadian engineers and pioneers started to reorganize the transportation links between the staging areas and the front and to construct artillery positions. In a short time, the transfer of huge amounts of ammunition and supplies to designated areas near the front-lines was underway.

Despite almost continuous German shelling, including deadly gas shells, the work continued apace. By October 25th, all the necessary preparations were finished and the Canadian Corps was ready to go over the top.

"We were led back to a "dump" where each man was told to take up and carry a section of new-made bath mats. All around the giant horseshoe of the Salient there were red flashes and winking glows, and the misty light of flares... Their fitful gleams made strange moving shadows over the swamp. A machine-gun fired nervously, and its bullets buried themselves with vicious thuds in jagged tree stubs close by. We hurried, then met the leading carriers returning. Each man as he came to the end of the bath mats we trod, threw down the one he was carrying, butting it to the one on which he stood. Thus the path grew with amazing speed. But the boards were new and their light colour was detected."

Will Bird, 42nd (Royal Highlanders) Battalion

The Canadian front-lines facing Passchendaele Ridge were split in two by the impassable morass that had once been the quaint valley of the Ravebeek River. Currie's decision to attack Passchendaele Ridge by launching a two-pronged offensive up the drier spurs dictated that the two assault forces be divided. The 3rd Canadian Division was ordered to capture the Bellevue Spur, located north of the remains of the Ravebeek Valley, and then to advance 1,200 metres towards the village of Passchendaele, the high point on the Ridge. South of the morass of the Ravebeek, the 4th Canadian Division, utilizing the foothold gained by the Australians as a jump off point, would begin its methodical ascent up Passchendaele Ridge.

On October 24th, the assault battalions moved forward to take up their positions in advance of the attack. They struggled through the mud and incessant shelling to reach the interconnected, water-filled shell holes which served as the front-line. The soldiers waited in the sodden trenches, trying to sleep, and hungrily eating whatever rations they had.

" To Your Health, Civilisation" by Louis Raemaekers
(Imperial War Museum)

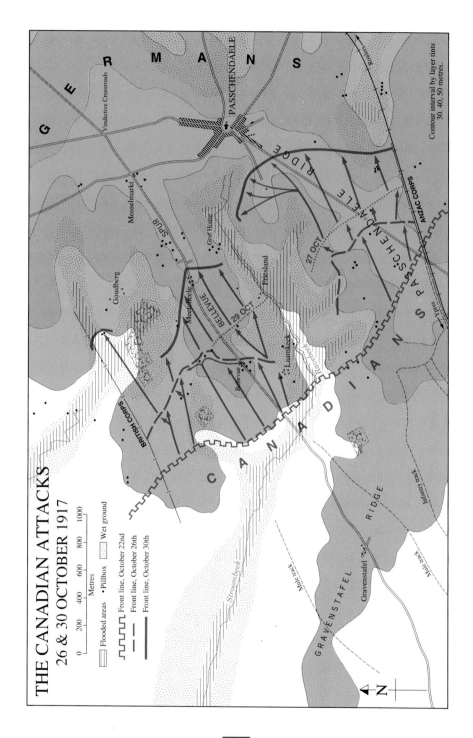

THE CANADIAN ATTACKS
26 & 30 OCTOBER 1917

Metres
0 200 400 600 800 1000

Flooded areas   • Pillbox   Wet ground

Front line, October 22nd
Front line, October 26th
Front line, October 30th

Contour interval by layer tints
30, 40, 50 metres.

GERMANS

PASSCHENDAELE

Vindictive Crossroads

Mosselmarkt

SPUR

Graf House

Goudberg

Meetcheele

BELLEVUE

Friesland

27 OCT

29 OCT

Bellevue

Laamkeek

PASSCHENDAELE SPUR

RIDGE

ANZAC CORPS

Ravebeek

BRITISH CORPS

CANADIAN

Roulers

Ypres

Stroombeek

Mule track

GRAVENSTAFEL

RIDGE

Gravenstafel

Infantry track

Mule track

N

THE FIRST PHASE: OCTOBER 26TH, 1917

The attack went in at 5:40 a.m. on October 26th. The battalions of the 3rd Division rose from their positions and advanced along the shattered remnants of the Gravenstafel-Passchendaele road toward the Bellevue Spur. Plodding forward in the thick mire, they captured the front-line German positions and pushed steadily forward. The Germans responded immediately with a deadly artillery bombardment. Initially, the Canadians held their gains, but the positions could not be defended and the shelling forced most of the Canadian soldiers to retire.

Throughout the battle for Passchendaele Ridge, individual feats of bravery saved situations that appeared lost. A group belonging to the 43rd Battalion, the Cameron Highlanders of Winnipeg, refused to relinquish its hard-won and valuable gains 700 metres up on the Bellevue Spur. Lieutenant Robert Shankland and his men fought off several German counter-attacks against immense odds. Shankland then returned to the old front-lines to obtain reinforcements. Under heavy fire, he led the reinforcements across the old No Man's Land to the isolated Canadians. Miraculously, the position held and Shankland won the Victoria Cross for his courage on Bellevue Spur that day.

Similar feats of bravery enabled two other Canadian battalions, the 52nd from Northern Ontario and the 4th Canadian Rifles of Central Ontario, to achieve significant gains against determined German resistance. Following Shankland's accomplishment, Major Chris O'Kelly and his company from the 52nd Battalion attacked and destroyed six German pillboxes that were blocking the Canadian advance. Private Tommy Holmes of the 4th Canadian Mounted Rifles similarly saved an untenable situation. When his unit was pinned down by furious German machine-gun fire, Holmes singlehandedly knocked out two machine-guns, captured a pillbox, took 19 German prisoners and opened the way for the 4th Canadian Mounted Rifles to press onward. Both O'Kelly and Holmes were awarded the Victoria Cross.

Despite these extraordinary acts of valour, the 3rd Division was unable to attain its limited objective on the first day of the offensive. But, at Passchendaele, any gains were respectable. The men dug in as best they could, trying to protect themselves from German machine-gun and artillery fire and prepared for the next phase of the assault. To the south, the 4th Division's attack, up the higher and drier Passchendaele Ridge, was

Arthur Currie was the most capable soldier that Canada has produced. Through his successes as the Commander of the Canadian Corps, Currie rose to international prominence beyond what has been achieved by any Canadian before or since. He was born in Strathroy, Ontario, on December 5, 1875. As an adult, he moved to British Columbia where he became involved in real estate. Like all good Canadian businessmen at the time, he joined the Canadian Militia and became the Commander of the 50th Gordon Highlanders. With the declaration of war in 1914, he eagerly joined the Canadian Expeditionary Force and fought with exceptional composure at Ypres in 1915 where his 2nd Brigade made a remarkable stand against the poison gas. Having impressed his superiors, Currie was promoted to command the "crack" 1st Canadian Division. He led the "Red Patch" at Mount Sorrel, through the horror of the Somme and guided it's momentous success at Vimy Ridge. In June 1917, Currie succeeded Julian Byng as Commander of the Canadian Corps. Over the next 17 months, Currie's Canadians won several decisive battles including the capture of Passchendaele Ridge, but it is for his classic victories at Amiens, Arras and Cambrai in 1918 that he is best known. The breaking of the formidable Drocourt-Queant line by Currie's Canadians is considered the greatest Allied success of the war.

General Sir Arthur Currie. Commander of the Canadian Corps 1917-19

Arthur Currie was tall, overweight and possessed a typically Canadian ability in using course language which certainly upset his more refined British superiors. He was also open-minded, pragmatic and careful with the lives of his soldiers, rare qualities in a First World War General. But it was his ability to organize, plan and execute which set him apart from all others. Currie could always "deliver the goods".

He returned to Canada in 1919 with little fanfare and later became the Principal of McGill University. Arthur Currie died in 1933. His funeral was a major event in Montreal and thousands lined the streets to honour the "Great Leader" of the Canadian Corps. He is buried in Mount Royal Cemetery, Montreal.

successful. By the end of the first day, they had inched the line almost one kilometre closer to the village of Passchendaele.

End of the First Phase: Gains 400-1,000 metres; Casualties 2,871, including 598 dead.

THE SECOND PHASE: OCTOBER 30TH, 1917

The exhausted soldiers were relieved by rested battalions that were to continue to push towards Passchendaele. The 3rd Division, now hanging on in shell-holes, was given the formidable task of capturing the remaining length of Bellevue Spur. The Germans knew the Bellevue Spur was the most important position defending Passchendaele Ridge and had placed numerous pillboxes at all the strategic locations along its entire span. Both the Canadians and Germans understood that the struggle for Bellevue Spur would be a fight to the finish.

To achieve its objective, the Commanders of the 3rd Division devised a frontal attack which they hoped would break the back of the stiff German resistance and lead to the capture of the entire Bellevue Spur. The 49th Battalion, comprised of Albertans, would drive up the remains of the Gravenstafel-Passchendaele road which followed the crest of the Spur. Their northern flank would be secured by the 5th Canadian Mounted Rifles from Quebec. To their immediate south, the Princess Patricia's Light Infantry (PPCLI), a battalion recruited from Eastern Ontario, would attack into the dense muck that had once been the beautiful Ravebeek Valley.

Simultaneous to the 3rd Division's assault up the Bellevue Spur, the 4th Division would also launch a three-pronged attack from the strong foothold it had established part way up Passchendaele Ridge. In the centre, the Winnipeg Grenadiers of the 78th Battalion would move forward across the ruined Passchendaele-Zonnebeke road. The Nova Scotia Highlanders would attack south of the road while the Seaforth Highlanders of Vancouver would move north from the road to capture the important German defences at Crest Farm, just west of Passchendaele village.

The Canadians had great difficulty determining where they were to attack. All landmarks shown on reference maps had been obliterated; roads, trees and most buildings were reduced to dust. Even the German pill boxes had been covered by the mud flash thrown up by exploding shells.

Nonetheless, the attack began at 5:50 a.m. on October 30th during a rain storm. Initially, all went well. However, heavy German opposition and artillery fire soon crushed the attacks of the PPCLI and the 49th Battalion.

Only individual acts of courage brought a measure of success to the attack. When a large German pillbox on the Gravenstafel-Passchendaele road held up the 3rd Division's attack, Lieutenant Hugh MacKenzie of the 7th Machine-Gun Company led a frontal assault on the position while a second group under Sergeant Harry Mullin of the PPCLI outflanked and captured the pillbox. Unfortunately, MacKenzie was killed during the frontal attack. Both men were awarded the Victoria Cross for their exceptional leadership and bravery. Despite the success of Mackenzie and Mullin, the PPCLI and the 49th were pinned down and throughout the day suffered severe losses for gains of about 500 metres. After the battle, the roll-call of the two battalions was a sorry sight. The PPCLI suffered 363 killed and wounded out of 600 attackers. The 49th from Edmonton lost 443 men out of the 588 who had gone into battle. More than three-quarters of the Albertans were casualties.

"I am still alright and hanging on. Our attack was successful but both it and holding have been awfully costly. Haggard, Papineau, Sulivan, Agar, Almon, Riddell, Williams, Morris, MacKenzie, killed... The ground we gained and held against two counter-attacks and continuing artillery bombardment is of some importance, as the ridge we took is a commanding one and I do not expect the Army thought we would be able to hold it, even if able to take it... but I cannot help wondering if the position gained was worth the awful sacrifice of life."
Agar Adamson, PPCLI

Agar Adamson, PPCLI

On the northern flank of the 3rd Division, the 5th Canadian Mounted Rifles led by Major George Pearkes performed the most courageous act of the battle and, in no small way, ensured the capture of Passchendaele. Pearkes was concerned that the British units, attacking beside the Canadians, would be unable to keep up with the momentum of the

Canadian advance. His solution to the problem was to allocate a group of his men to capture strategic Source Farm which was in the British sphere of operation.

Advancing against heavy machine-gun fire and across open ground, the 5th Canadian Mounted Rifles attacked in small groups and not only successfully captured Source Farm, but also held out against many determined German counter-attacks. Given the circumstances, it seems incomprehensible how these small groups thwarted the persistent German attacks. Undoubtedly, this action saved the men of the 49th Battalion and the PPCLI from total destruction and ensured the capture of Passchendaele village in the near future. It was one of the bravest small-group actions by Canadians in the entire First World War. Pearkes was awarded the Victoria Cross for leading this crucial attack.

"The vast field of shell-holes had been turned into a sea of mud by the heavy rain of the last few days... On my zigzag course I passed many a lonely and forgotten corpse. Often only a head or a hand projected from the shell-hole whose circle of dirty water reflected them. Thousands sleep like that, without one token of love to mark the unknown grave."
Ernst Junger, German Army

As night fell on October 30th, confusion was everywhere. The Canadian Generals had no idea where the front-line positions were located nor how many men were defending the costly gains. The potential existed for a well-organized German counter-attack that could obliterate the Canadians. As a result, the night of October 30th-31st passed precariously. Reinforcements were moved up and gradually the gains were solidified. The 3rd Division was short of its objective and had paid a very heavy price for the additional ground acquired, but they had advanced the line further up Bellevue Spur and were now on drier ground.

The 4th Division's attack on the Passchendaele Ridge went according to plan. Although suffering heavy casualties, the soldiers from Nova Scotia had advanced and captured a series of fortified buildings near Passchendaele. But it was a bittersweet victory for the Nova Scotians who suffered their worst day of the war losing 439 killed and wounded. The 78th Battalion from Winnipeg had succeeded on their flank and the 72nd, of Vancouver, also completed its difficult task and captured Crest Farm. In sweeping the Germans from Crest Farm, the men from British Columbia had displayed exceptional bravery and efficiency. Passchendaele village was now less than 100 metres away.
Phase Two: Gains 300 to 900 metres; Casualties 2,321, including 884 dead.

"In another bit of old trench, where the parados had disappeared, a soldier stood rigidly, feet braced apart. He had been killed by concussion, and his body was split as if sliced by a great knife. Some German bodies were lying on a bank and one, bare-headed, looked as if he were reclining on one elbow."

Will Bird, 42nd
(Royal Highlanders) Battalion

Will Bird

THE THIRD PHASE: THE CAPTURE OF PASSCHENDAELE, NOVEMBER 6TH, 1917

After the ferocious fighting surrounding the attacks of October 30th, the depleted battalions of the 3rd and 4th Canadian Divisions were withdrawn from the battle. Their replacements were the fresh soldiers of their sister Divisions, the 1st and 2nd. The Canadians were now well up on Passchendaele Ridge and on drier land. When the assault was renewed by the 1st and 2nd Divisions on November 6th, the remains of the village of Passchendaele were certain to fall. The honour of capturing the "infamous" village was to belong to the 2nd Division; the 1st Division, emerging from the Bellevue Spur, was to attack Passchendaele Ridge north of the village.

"We were everywhere pressing on the heels of death... Here lay a group behind a tattered hedge, their bodies covered by the still fresh earth that showered on them after the shell had burst; there, two runners near a shell hole, from which the suffocating vapour of the explosives still exhaled. At other spots there were many corpses scattered over a small surface..."

Ernst Junger, German Army

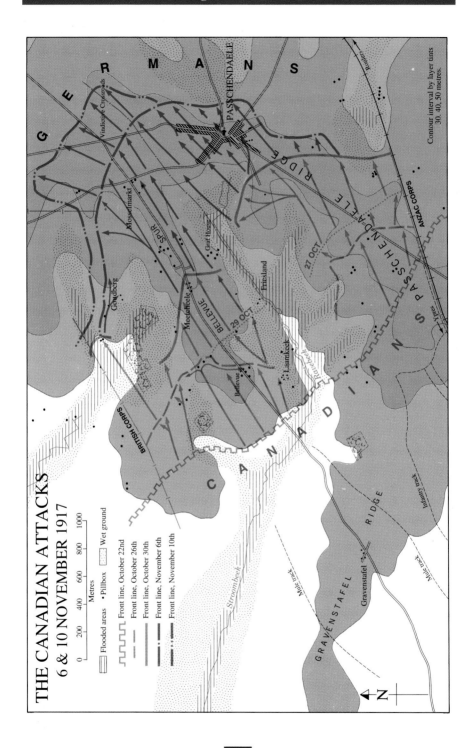

THE CANADIAN ATTACKS
6 & 10 NOVEMBER 1917

Metres

0   200   400   600   800   1000

☐ Flooded areas   • Pillbox   ☐ Wet ground

ↆↆↆↆ Front line, October 22nd

– – – Front line, October 26th

——— Front line, October 30th

—·—· Front line, November 6th

—··—·· Front line, November 10th

Contour interval by layer tints
30, 40, 50 metres.

GERMANS

PASSCHENDAELE

PASSCHENDAELE RIDGE

Vindictive Crossroads

Mosselmarkt

SPUR

Graf Housz

Goudberg

Meetcheele

BELLEVUE

Bellevue

Friesland

Laamkeek

Ravebeek

21 OCT

29 OCT

ANZAC CORPS

Ypres

PASS

SCHEND

CANADIANS

BRITISH CORPS

Stroombeek

Mule track

GRAVENSTAFEL

Gravenstafel

RIDGE

Mule track

Infantry track

N

From the beginning, almost everything went according to plan. By 6:00 a.m., the 1st Division had stormed Passchendaele Ridge north of the village. In a spirited action, the 3rd Battalion from Toronto protected the northern flank of the assault by seizing a fortified farm which was pouring machine-gun fire into the Canadian attack. Private Colin Barron, in a feat of remarkable bravery, captured three enemy machine-gun posts enabling his battalion to secure the position. He was awarded the Victoria Cross. The whole attack by the 1st Division was a huge success. The fact it was launched from the drier ground was a major reason for the victory.

The 2nd Division's assault on the shattered remains of Passchendaele village was also remarkably successful. The 27th Battalion, recruited from the city of Winnipeg, was given the task of liberating the village. Fighting was often hand-to-hand as the Germans tried desperately to hang on. At a critical juncture in the battle, Private James Robertson destroyed an important German machine-gun post, opening the way for his comrades to enter the village. Robertson, who was later killed, was awarded the Victoria Cross posthumously. After the bloody fighting, Passchendaele was finally in the hands of the men from Winnipeg. All that was left of the village was smashed brick and dust.

The 31st Battalion from Alberta and the 28th Battalion from Saskatchewan had also succeeded. They had charged out of the Ravebeek Valley to capture the area of Passchendaele Ridge just north of the village and had then linked-up with the men of the 1st Division. Everywhere, the Canadians were victorious. The offensive to capture Passchendaele had started on July 31st, 1917. It had taken the Allies more than 98 days and 250,000 casualties to reach the village and the dubious honour of taking it had fallen to the Canadians.

Phase Three: Gains 1,000 metres; Casualties 2,238 including 734 dead.

"Then I started to walk up the terrible, muddy roads till I came to the different German pill-boxes which had been converted into headquarters for the battalions. Finally, after wading through water and mud nearly up to my knees, I found myself the next afternoon wandering near Goudberg Copse, with a clear view of the ruins of Passchendaele, which was held by another division on our right. The whole region was unspeakably horrible. Rain was falling, the dreary waste of shell-ploughed mud, yellow and clinging, stretched off into the distance as far as the eye could see. Bearer parties, tired and pale, were carrying out the wounded on stretchers, making a journey of several miles in doing so. The bodies of dead men lay here and there where they had fallen in the advance. I came across one poor boy who had been killed that morning. His

Frederick Scott

body was covered with a shiny coating of yellow mud, and looked like a statue made of bronze. He had a beautiful face, with finely shaped head covered with close, curling hair, and looked more like some work of art than a human being. The huge shell holes were half full of water often reddened with human blood, and many of the wounded had rolled down in the pools and been drowned. As I went on, someone I met told me that there was a wounded man in the trenches ahead of me.

"I made my way in the direction indicated and shouted out asking if anybody was there. Suddenly I heard a faint voice replying, and I hurried to the place from which the sound came. There I found sitting up in the mud of the trench, his legs almost covered with water, a lad who told me that he had been there for many hours. I never saw anything like the wonderful expression on his face. He was smiling most cheerfully, and made no complaint about what he had suffered. I told him I would get a stretcher, so I went to some trenches not far away and got a bearer party and a stretcher and went over to rescue him. The men jumped down into the trench and moved him very gently, but his legs were so numb that although they were hit he felt no pain. One of the men asked him if he was hit in the legs. He said, "Yes," but the man looked up at me and pulling up the boy's tunic showed me a hideous wound in his back."

Chaplain Frederick Scott, 1st Canadian Division

"The Harvest of Battle" by C.R.W. Nevinson (Imperial War Museum)

THE FOURTH PHASE: NOVEMBER 10TH, 1917.

The Canadians were now firmly established on top of Passchendaele Ridge. However, the Germans were still clinging to the slopes east of the village. On November 10th, the final Canadian attack was launched to secure their hard-won position on the Ridge. North of the village, the 1st Division successfully captured the German positions and drove the enemy eastwards on to the flat plain below. On their southern flank, the 2nd Division also succeeded in pushing the Germans off the eastern slopes.

The view of rolling, green countryside to the east must have seemed like heaven to the advancing Canadian troops, for the view westward, toward Ypres, was that of hell.

Phase Four: Gains 1,000 metres; Casualties 1,094, including 420 dead.

THE BATTLE ENDS

The Third Battle of Ypres ended with the attack of November 10th. It had cost the British Empire more than 250,000 dead, wounded and missing. The price the Canadians paid for their two-week tenure in the mud at Passchendaele was more than 5,000 lives. All told, 16,000 Canadians were killed, wounded and missing.

The Canadians held the line at Passchendaele until mid-November when they were withdrawn to the Vimy-Lens sector. It was their last visit to the immortal Ypres salient. They had fought there in 1915 at Second Ypres, in 1916 at Mount Sorrel and now at Passchendaele. They had left more than 15,000 of their comrades in the soil of Flanders.

CONCLUSION

In a war where slaughter was commonplace, Passchendaele was a hideous battle. Time and again, soldiers struggled through the thick ooze with little cover to attack strongly fortified positions knowing the odds of dying or being seriously wounded were very great. Men drowned in the liquefied Flanders Plain. The wounded suffered enormously and it often took six stretcher-bearers to carry them to the pick-up points.

Squire nagged and bullied till I went to fight,
(Under Lord Derby's Scheme). I died in hell -
(They called it Passchendaele). My wound was slight,
And I was hobbling back: and then a shell
Burst slick upon the duck-boards: so I fell
Into the bottomless mud, and lost the light.

Siegfried Sassoon

Did the battle of Passchendaele serve a purpose? Even the defenders of the battle admit the objective of capturing the channel ports was unrealistic. The only argument they offer in support of the slaughter is that, in a war of attrition, Germany, with a smaller population than the Allies, could not afford to replace its losses. This is true. The Germans did not have the men, but the champions of the Passchendaele cause fail to recognize that the battle bled the British Army as well and contributed to its collapse during the German offensives in 1918. The promoters of the war of attrition also overlook the suffering incurred by the thousands of families who lost a loved one in this awful battle.

For Canada, Passchendaele proved that Canadian troops were the best the British Empire had to offer. They had fought with immense determination and courage and had won a victory few thought possible. In 1917, the Canadians had succeeded when all others failed. They had triumphed at Vimy, Arleux, Fresnoy and now were the victors at Passchendaele. In the worst year of the war for the Allies, it was the Canadians who had come through.

The saddest part of the battle, won at such a huge cost by the Canadians, was how insignificant Passchendaele was to the overall outcome of the war. In 1918, during the German offensive at Ypres, Passchendaele was surrendered without a fight.

All the arguments made by the supporters and detractors of Passchendaele cannot touch the true cost of war. It is the personal grief; the loss of a son, a brother, a husband, that makes war so tragic. Caroline Papineau could not cope with the death of her beloved son, Talbot. She wrote to Agar Adamson after the battle:

"The courage and regiment with which he faced what I am told was a well desperate attack, fills my heart with pride, but also with bitterness - I've nothing. Nothing can console me for the loss of my boy who had been the joy and comfort of my life." ∎

24

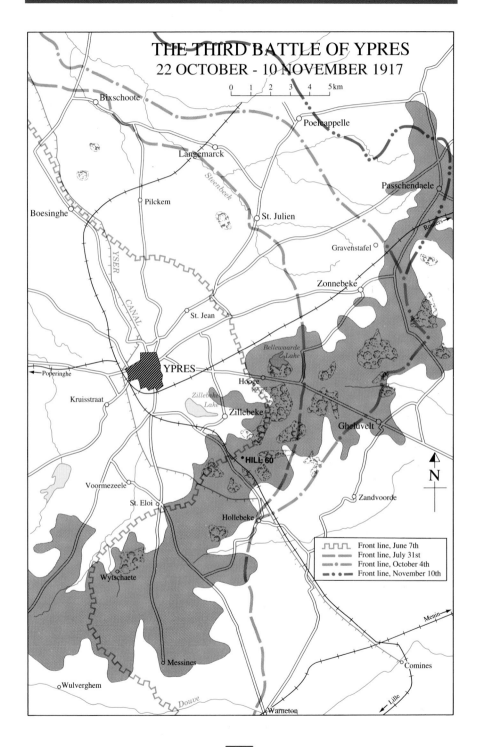

THE THIRD BATTLE OF YPRES
22 OCTOBER - 10 NOVEMBER 1917

0   1   2   3   4   5 km

Bixschoote

Poelcappelle

Langemarck

Steenbeek

Passchendaele

Pilckem

Boesinghe

St. Julien

Rollers

Gravenstafel

Zonnebeke

YSER

CANAL

St. Jean

Bellewaarde Lake

← Poperinghe

YPRES

Hooge

Zillebeke Lake

Kruisstraat

Zillebeke

Gheluvelt

• HILL 60

N

Voormezeele

Zandvoorde

St. Eloi

Hollebeke

Menin →

⌐⌐⌐⌐⌐ Front line, June 7th
— — — Front line, July 31st
—·—·— Front line, October 4th
•••••• Front line, November 10th

Wytschaete

Messines

Comines

Wulverghem

Douve

Lille →

Warneton

TALBOT PAPINEAU

Born into a privileged and famous family at Montebello, Quebec, on March 25th, 1883, Talbot Mercer Papineau was undoubtedly destined for a distinguished political career. His unfortunate fate, however, was a premature and altogether undistinguished end in the mud of Passchendaele, a victim of his own father's generation.

He was the son of Louis-Joseph Papineau and an American, Caroline Rogers of Philadelphia, and the grandson of Louis-Joseph Papineau, leader of the famed Lower Canada Rebellion of 1837. A product of two cultures, Papineau became the perfect, anglicized French Canadian. Educated at McGill and later, as a Rhodes Scholar, at Oxford, he was typical of the Canadian elite of the era.

Setting himself up for a political career, he started his own law practice in Montreal where his family and social connections

Talbot Mercer Papineau

quickly aided his ambitions. Politically, Papineau's views were modern, more those of a Canadian Nationalist than a supporter of the British Empire. His family's wealth allowed him the freedom to do as he pleased and hard work was an unlikely requirement to help him along his chosen path.

With the declaration of war in August 1914, the 31 year-old bachelor rushed to join the privately-raised Princess Patricia's Canadian Light Infantry (PPCLI), a regiment financed by his good friend Hamilton Gault of Montreal. Papineau easily received a commission and served with the PPCLI in France beginning in February 1915.

He was awarded the Military Cross for bravery during a trench raid at St. Eloi, Belgium on February 27th and survived the grim battle at Bellewaerde Ridge on May 8th, where the PPCLI suffered 397 casualties.

Then, in late 1915, suffering from "battle fatigue," Papineau was invalided to a hospital on the coast of France. In February 1916, he took a staff appointment behind the lines. Always conscious of appearances, he knew he was helping his career in many ways, but did not like the fact many of his fellow officers would see him as "windy."

In 1916, through the battles of Mount Sorrel and the Somme, the PPCLI suffered heavily while Papineau survived safely behind the front and watched the fates of his comrades. At this point, he became embroiled in the public debate over the role of French Canada in the war. But he knew it was easy to talk about the need for sacrifice when he was a long way from the actual fighting.

In 1917, his old regiment was successfully involved in the capture of Vimy Ridge on April 9th. This was a great day for Canada and Papineau, once again, was aware of his distance from the action. Mindful of how this might hurt his future political ambitions, he finally decided to return to the Patricias in May of that year.

At 5:50 a.m. on October 30th, 1917, the Canadians attacked in the awful mud of Passchendaele and, minutes later, Talbot Mercer Papineau was instantly killed by a direct hit from a German shell. His last words were, "Hughie, this is suicide." Papineau may be remembered for fighting in the PPCLI's worst battle of the war. The regiment suffered 363 killed, wounded and missing for an insignificant advance against the Germans. There was no time to bury the dead and Papineau was among the many left unburied. A few weeks later, a PPCLI party found "a pair of feet with reversed putties was seen sticking out of a shell hole full of water . . . Major Papineau always wore his putties that way. They pulled the body out and, by examining the contents of the pockets, found it to be Papineau. Part of a shell had hit him in the stomach blowing everything else above away, poor fellow. He could not have known what hit him."

A cross was placed over the remains but, in 1919, when the battlefields were cleared, only the cross was found.

Talbot Papineau, with all his hopes and dreams, is commemorated by name only on the Menin Gate Memorial in Ypres. ∎

THE BODY SNATCHERS

No war prior to 1914 had killed as many men as did the First World War. More than 1.1 million British Commonwealth soldiers died! In a unique decision, the Government of Great Britain passed a law that all the Fallen would remain in the country where they died. Beautiful cemeteries would be constructed and each designed as an Edwardian garden. The men would lie with their comrades; there would be no distinction of rank; all would be equal in death. The cemeteries would memorialize their sacrifice and future generations would remember their legacy. It was a beautiful concept, based on pride and honour. Few could argue against it. But to achieve these lofty goals, no bodies could be returned to their home countries.

For many, not being able to bring the body of their loved one home was a bitter disappointment. Most of the families could not afford to visit the graves in Europe and they could not complete the grieving process. For many the pain of losing a son or a husband would only be satisfied by a proper burial in the family plot at home. Repatriating the bodies was against the law, but for some the grief was too great to be deterred.

One such mother was Anna Durie of George Street in Toronto. Anna's only son, William Arthur Peel Durie, was born in Toronto in 1881. His father was the influential

William Arthur Peel Durie

Dr. William Durie. In 1885, the Doctor died suddenly and the life of Anna Durie became her only son. William attended the best schools and moved in the elite social circles of Toronto. Like many affluent gentlemen of his era, Durie took up a career in banking and won a commission in the local militia unit, the 36th Peel Regiment.

In 1915, the 34 year-old enlisted in the 58th Canadian Infantry Battalion and went to France in March 1916. On May 4th, he was seriously wounded by a sniper's bullet and almost died of his wounds. Miraculously, he recovered and rejoined his unit in France in December. On December 29th, 1917, in the frontline trenches near Lens, a large trench mortar shell hit the parados, killing Durie instantly. Subsequently, he was buried in Corkscrew British Cemetery near Lens, France. His mother was devastated by his loss. Her whole world was destroyed.

In 1919, she approached the Imperial, now Commonwealth, War Graves Commission (CWGC) and requested the repatriation of her son's body. Her application was, of course, rejected. In August 1921, resolved to bring the remains home to Canada, Anna, her daughter and a Frenchman made an unsuccessful, nocturnal attempt to remove the body from the cemetery.

During August 1925, when all the graves in Corkscrew Cemetery were exhumed and moved to Loos British Cemetery, Anna took advantage of the shuffle to remove her son's coffin. Although the ground disturbance was noted by the CWGC, a ground probe determined the coffin to still be there. The CWGC did not find out about Anna's successful exhumation of the body and its return to Canada until a newspaper reported the reburial.

Her son's grave is in St. James Cemetery, Toronto. He was buried with full military honours with ex-soldiers of the 58th Canadian Infantry Battalion in uniform attending the ceremony.

What brought Anna to France also brought many other families to France and Belgium during the 1920s to search the battlefields for the lost grave of a loved one. Learning a husband or son was "missing" only exacerbated the tragedy and sorrow brought to more than a million British Commonwealth families by the First World War. Of the 1,115,000 Commonwealth dead, of whom 66,000 were Canadians, more than 530,000 had no known grave. Under the terms of the CWGC, no bodies were permitted to leave the country in which the man had died. For Canadian families, then, few of their loved ones would be buried at home.

Some families were not satisfied with this condition and applied for repatriation of the body. The application was always referred and ultimately rejected. The alternative left to the bereaved family was to steal the body from the military cemetery and ship it home for reburial. Between 1919 and 1925, under the auspices of the CWGC, the battlefields were scoured for missing bodies. As a result, hundreds of thousands of bodies were dug up and reburied in war cemeteries. Old battlefields still scarred the countryside and the chances of getting away with a clandestine operation were great. Local help could even be purchased to assist.

It is not known and is difficult to estimate how many bodies were removed in this fashion. CWGC records indicate only six such thefts, but appear to overlook others, for example, the famous heist of the South African Fighter Ace Captain Andrew Beauchamp-Proctor VC, DSO, MC, DFC from his original grave in England. Of the six recorded thefts, of which three were Canadian, four were successful.

Private Grenville Hopkins of the Princess Patricia's Canadian Light Infantry (PPCLI) was killed November 15th, 1917. In 1920, an unmarked grave containing two bodies was found north of Passchendaele village. The two were Private Granville Hopkins and Private McKeown, also of the PPCLI. The father of Private Hopkins identified the remains of his son. In January 1921, the family applied for repatriation of his remains, but the application was denied. On the night of May 17th-18th, 1921, the body was removed and the theft discovered the next morning. The Belgian authorities were alerted and the body was found in the mortuary in Antwerpen and reclaimed. Private Hopkins is now buried in Schoonselhof Cemetery in Belgium. His parents are long dead.

Major Charles Sutcliffe, a Canadian in the Royal Flying Corps, was killed June 6th, 1917, and buried in Epinoy Churchyard in France. In August 1925, a man, accompanied by Sutcliffe's father, had the body exhumed and taken to Canada. Major Sutcliffe is now buried in Lindsay, Ontario.

The question of repatriation of remains is even an issue today. Only the Australians have been successful in circumventing the rigid rules. After the First World War, the remains of Major General Sir William Bridges, KCB, CMU were removed from his burial place in Egypt to Australia. In 1994, the Australian government took home an unknown soldier from a CWGC cemetery in France. The soldier was reburied in Canberra, the Capital of Australia, and is Australia's "Unknown Soldier", representing all Australians killed in war. Canada does not have an Unknown Soldier.

Other countries have been less successful. The Israeli government has tried unsuccessfully to repatriate men of the Palestine Regiment killed in Italy during the Second World War. Fiji failed in its attempt to return the body of a Fijian Victoria Cross winner from a cemetery in Papua, New Guinea.

In the 1970s, the Republic of Ireland requested the repatriation of three soldiers of the Connaught Rangers, buried in India, whose graves had been abandoned by the CWGC. As the graves were no longer within the jurisdiction of the CWGC, the remains of all three were returned to Ireland and reburied as heroes of the Irish Nationalist cause!

In general, the bodies of Commonwealth soldiers killed in the two World Wars, rest where they died in more than 150 countries around the world. Many of their graves have never been visited by their families and they lie forgotten in beautiful cemeteries, now far away in time and distance. The grieving families, themselves have mostly died off, but it is difficult not to feel the sadness of so long ago. One mother expressed her grief by including a sad inscription on her son's grave: "Oh for the touch of a vanished hand, and the sound of a voice so still."

Anna Durie joined her husband and her son in St.James Cemetery in 1933. ■

CANADIAN INDIANS

Chris Silversmith was typical of many Canadian Indians who served in the Great War. He was born on the Six Nations Reserve at Caledonia, Ontario. The date of birth was never recorded, but he was apparently 26 years old when he enlisted in 1916 with the 114th Battalion at Caledonia. His enlistment documents indicate the strapping 6'3" Silversmith's religion as "Long House - Pagan" and it is clear the enthusiastic farmer could not sign his own name. His complexion was noted as "dark Indian", his hair "black", and his eyes "very dark".

Chris Silversmith

One-half of the 114th and the 107th Battalion of Winnipeg were made up of Indian recruits. Clearly sympathetic to the Canadian Indians, the officers of the 114th still had that age-old, unmalicious

31

prejudice against inferior races so prevalent in the British Empire. However, unlike other races, the Canadian Indians were recruited with genuine enthusiasm because of their reputation as a daring and loyal "warrior" breed.

Most of the 3,500 Indians who enlisted were scattered throughout the forces. They represented tribes from across Canada including the Micmacs, Mohawks, Onondagas, Oneidas, Tuscaroras, Delawares, Chippewas, Sioux, Bloods, Okanagan, Peguis, Saulteaux and Crees. Among the Indian enlistments were: the famous long-distance runner Tom Longboat; Cameron Brant, great grandson of Joseph Brant; and Patrick Riel, grandson of the Metis leader Louis Riel.

Once in England, the 114th Battalion was broken up for reinforcements and sent to France piecemeal. Silversmith was sent to the 107th Canadian Pioneer Battalion and fought in the battles of Passchendaele and Hill 70, where he was wounded. Others served as snipers or scouts. Henry Norwest was considered to be the greatest sniper in the British Army and was credited with 115 "observed" hits.

Although clearly successful soldiers, the "lesser race" prejudice remained. When the Military Service Act was introduced in 1917, the Indians were excluded because they were "wards of the Government and, as such, minors in the eyes of the law, and that, as they had not the right to exercise the franchise or other privileges of citizenship, they should not be expected responsibilities equal to those of enfranchised persons."

Nonetheless, more than 35% of eligible Canadian Indians enlisted, a remarkable percentage! By the end of the war, they had won 30 awards for bravery. The most decorated of all was Francis Pegahmagabow of Parry Sound who was awarded the Military Medal three times. They had also instilled fear in the enemy. Legends of Indian stealth, cunning and ferocity were world-renowned.

"...the English were all over us. I walked up the steps behind a corporal who was very defiant and he spat on the floor... but this did him no good for he was hit over the head by a huge tommy who was brandishing a baseball bat... Looking at the soldiers I noticed that they all had their faces blackened... One of the soldiers wore no helmet and had no hair apart from a small tuft on the top of his head. He also had white and red paint on his face and was very fearsome looking. I then realized he was a Red Indian, and our captors were Canadian.

Anonymous German soldier

Unfortunately, more than 320 Canadian Indians died in the war or as a result of war injuries. The first to fall was Cameron Brant, killed at Ypres in 1915. Patrick Riel fell late in 1915, the victim of a sniper's bullet. Even Henry Norwest, the intrepid sniper, was finally sniped himself in August 1918. The revered marksman was buried by his comrades in Warvillers Churchyard, east of Amiens.

Like other Canadian soldiers, these men returned to Canada in 1919 to a strangely different world. In the series, "Canada in the Great War," the following passage expresses their future hopes:

"The unselfish loyalty, gallantry, intelligence, resourcefulness and efficiency displayed by Indians from all nine provinces of Canada should throw a new light upon the sterling qualities of a race whose virtues are perhaps not sufficiently known or appreciated.

"The Indians themselves moreover cannot but feel an increased and renewed pride of race and self-respect that should ensure the recovery of that ancient dignity and independence of spirit that were unfortunately lost to them in some measure through the depletion of the game supply, their natural source of livelihood and the ravages of vices that had no place in their life before the advent of the white man.

"The Indians deserve well of Canada and the end of the war should mark the beginning of a new era for them wherein they shall play an increasingly honourable and useful part in the history of a country once the free and open hunting ground of their forefathers."

Silversmith was injured in 1918 and evacuated to England. He returned to Caledonia in May 1919, but fell ill and his death on March 25th, 1923, was attributed to war service. He was buried at Cayaga Long House Reserve, Caledonia. He left a wife, Catharine, and two daughters, Ida and Emiline. He was "apparently" 33 years old. ■

Militarism's Boarder on War Rations

Drawn by Sven Larsson

CONSCRIPTION

In the early morning of August 26th, 1918, the 2nd Canadian Mounted Rifles launched an attack against the German trenches on Orange Hill. Their attack was successful and the 2nd CMR advanced quickly with light casualties.

Private William Johnson participated in the initial attack and the pursuit of the Germans to Monchy. In the confusion of the battle, Johnson and two comrades went a short distance beyond the objective. The three took shelter in a shell-hole to avoid ferocious German machine-gun fire, but Johnson's head was exposed and a bullet passed through his forehead, killing him instantly.

William Douglas Johnson was born in Bracebridge, Ontario, in 1897, the son of Thomas and Amelia Johnson. In 1917, before joining the Colours, he was attending Law School. William Johnson had arrived in France on August 15th, 1918. His contribution to the Great War lasted only 11 days!

In many ways, William Johnson was no different than the 50,000 Canadian soldiers who had died before him. He was 5' 4½" tall, a Methodist and clearly the son of proud parents. But, in one way, William Johnson was quite different. He was not a volunteer; he was a conscript.

Few issues in Canadian politics have been as divisive as conscription. The First World War had drawn hundreds of thousands of volunteers into the ranks of Canada's army and navy, but many Canadian-born men remained reluctant to enlist and join the fighting overseas. The first Canadian contingents to cross the Atlantic had been predominantly British-born and Canada's manpower contribution to the war effort was proportionately lower than that of Great Britain, Australia and New Zealand.

The Canadian Prime Minister, Sir Robert Borden, had visited the Canadian Corps in March 1917. He was, at that time, staunchly against conscription, but Borden had been convinced by the faces of the Canadian soldiers in France that more help was needed. On his return to Canada, Borden, determined to raise 100,000 more men for the Canadian Corps, set to work on a bill that would make military service mandatory for Canadian males aged 20 to 44. However, the Military Service Act was vehemently opposed by the opposition Liberals under Laurier and Borden was forced to call a General Election.

The issue over conscription was clearly a problem. Not only had English-Canadians not enlisted with the same eagerness as their compatriots in other countries of the British Empire, they resented French-Canada for responding even less. Borden then made the divisive issue even worse by trying to fix the election by disenfranchising some Canadians, enfranchising others and allowing any Canadian soldier overseas to cast votes in any constituency. Borden's manipulations were not necessary and he won an overwhelming majority.

In August 1917, the Military Service Act had called for the registration of all eligible men. They were divided into six classes from Class 1, unmarried men between the ages of 20 and 45, to Class 6, married men between the ages of 40 and 44. By the end of all the wrangling and bureaucratic shuffling, 400,000 Class 1 men were registered; 220,000 of these were exempted from performing military service and 24,000 were defaulted for various reasons. The net result was 100,000 men were conscripted into the Canadian Forces; 47,000 went overseas, but only 24,000 served in France before the Armistice.

The first conscripts arrived in France in mid-August, 1918, and were quickly sent in to reinforce the front-line battalions after their losses at Amiens and Arras. One of those men was William Douglas Johnson.

His headstone in Monchy British Cemetery bears the high service number (3033865) characteristic of many of the MSA men. A poignant inscription at the base of his headstone marks his memory, one of the first conscripts to die; "FAITHFUL UNTO DEATH." ∎

BIBLIOGRAPHY - SUGGESTED READING

Legacy of Valour by D.Dancocks: Hurtig Publishers, 1986.

Ghosts Have Warm Hands by Will. R. Bird: CEF BOOKS, 1997.

Tapestry of War by Sandra Gwyn: Harper Collins Publishers, 1992.

Letters of Agar Adamson edited by N.M.Christie: CEF BOOKS, 1997.

The Official History of the Canadian Expeditionary Force, 1914-1919 by G.W.L.Nicholson: The Queen's Printer, 1962.

The Canadians at Passchendaele, October to November 1917 by Norm Christie: CEF BOOKS, 1996.

The Journal of Private Fraser edited by Dr. R.H. Roy: CEF BOOKS, 1998.